Drink Me
CURIOUS COCKTAILS FROM WONDERLAND

NICK PERRY

and PAUL ROSSER

ROCK POINT

Text © 2018 by Nick Perry

Photography and Illustrations © 2018 by Shutterstock

First published in 2018 by Rock Point,
an imprint of The Quarto Group
142 West 36th Street, 4th Floor
New York, NY 10018 USA
T (212) 779-4972 **F** (212) 779-6058
www.QuartoKnows.com

Rock Point titles are also available at discount for retail, wholesale, promotional, and bulk purchase. For details, contact the Special Sales Manager by email at specialsales@quarto.com or by mail at The Quarto Group, Attn: Special Sales Manager, 401 Second Avenue North, Suite 310, Minneapolis, MN 55401, USA.

10 9 8 7 6 5 4 3 2 1

ISBN: 978-1-63106-512-5

Editorial Director: Rage Kindelsperger
Managing Editor: Erin Canning
Aquiring Editor: John Foster
Cover and Interior Design: theBookDesigners

Printed in China

CONTENTS

PART I

INTRODUCTION

*L*ewis *Carroll's books* have always lent themselves to the fantastical, the unusual, and the strange. His magical growth potions, tea parties, and the like are the ultimate in gastronomic inspiration and we believe we have compiled a selection of recipes that tap into the rich vein of creative stimuli at play in Wonderland.

We discovered that there was no real resource available that catered to the demands of an Alice fan who wanted to create a boozy tea party. That's what this book aims to do. Come with us down the rabbit hole as we take you on a journey through our minds, showing you how to make some weird and wonderful creations. From basic cocktail-making techniques to more complex liquor-infusion methods, this book contains recipes to interest everyone, from a teetotalling Alice novice to a raving Alice fan or cocktail nut!

All great adventures start with a drink, and Alice's expedition down the rabbit hole is no exception. The story begins with a sip of a curiously labeled tipple.

The potion causes her to shrink to a minute size and is the catalyst for all that is to come. Here we invite you to do the same—learn how to mix cocktails that will fill you with wonder and glee at the flavor combinations, while amassing the perfect selection of drinks to bring together in your own spirit-soaked Mad Hatter's Tea Party. We have delved into the depths of the pool of tears in search of the most magical ingredients and sumptuous flavors, and after some sage advice from a helpful caterpillar, have composed a list of recipes we feel are regularly enjoyed by the inhabitants of Wonderland.

After an introduction that covers the basics on spirits, liqueurs, glassware, and techniques in Part I, we have concocted drinks—in a purposeful, unorderly Wonderland sequence—for every occasion and for all palates in Part II, no matter your drinking predilection. Perfect pre-dinner aperitifs are in abundance with the Queen of Hearts (page 66), a sweet, refreshing drink with bitter undertones, or the Painting the Roses Red (page 64), a bubbly highball of sharp raspberry and gin flavors, softened with a hint of rosewater. We explore the hallucinogenic properties of absinthe in our ode to the unknown, The Mushroom (page 56), a strong mix of aniseed, rose, and complex herbal flavors, while we reminisce over the taste of our childhood with recipes such as Bread-and-Butterfly Pudding (page 80) and the Un-Birthday Cake Martini (page 84). The Duchess's Soup (page 60) is a refined take on the punch bowl, and we make a refreshing palate cleanser in the form of The Caucus Chaser (page 48), a sticky plum and chestnut sharpener low enough in alcohol that you can greedily gulp it without even a hint of regret.

To supplement the core cocktail recipes, we have also created a list of lovingly crafted batch recipes in Part III to add to your pantry. They will serve as the base components to some of the curious cocktails you will discover in this book that you can prepare in advance and store in your cupboard or refrigerator, ready to use whenever you desire. So stock up with fabulous homemade vermouths, liqueurs, syrups, go ahead and enjoy exploring the landscape of the curious cocktails of Wonderland and beyond—and when presented with the opportunity, always remember: Drink me!

Spirits and Liqueurs

The world of spirits and liqueurs is a constantly growing beast, with new and unique products entering the market constantly. Here we will focus on the best-known and most popular spirit categories, their flavors and characteristics, and how they can best be used in drinks.

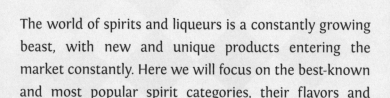

BRANDY

Made from distilled fruit, usually grapes, and sometimes plums or apples, brandy is made across the world. Many countries have their own styles, including Cognac, Armagnac, Calvados, Pisco, Grappa, Eau de Vie, Aquavit, Slivovice, and Schnapps/Snaps. Examples of its use in mixed drinks include classics such as the sour Sidecar, the creamy Brandy Alexander, and the elegant Champagne Cocktail. We enjoy a good-quality brandy served straight up, in a warmed brandy balloon glass, but the depth of burnt fruit flavor found in brandies works rather well in cocktails.

GIN

Gin is made from distilled grains, then flavored with an infinite variety of fruits, herbs, and spices, collectively known as botanicals. Juniper is the defining flavor of gin, in what must be the spirit world's largest flavor spectrum.

RUM

Made from distilled sugar, rum is generally quite sweet in nature. This makes it ideal to mix, and understandably there are a great number of recipes in which it stars, ranging from classics through to tiki-style cocktails and even the odd hot beverage. Rum is wide-ranging in varieties, from light, gold, and dark, through to Cachaça, flavored and spiced to overproof and navy strength.

TEQUILA

Tequila is distilled from the blue agave plant and made only in Mexico. Tightly regulated similar spirits without the required ratio of blue agave are known as mezcal and are smokier in flavor.

VODKA

Typically distilled from grains, vodka can be made from many things, including potatoes, grapes, and even milk! Generally odorless and neutral in flavor, vodka is one of the easiest liquors to blend into a cocktail, and a very popular spirit to flavor at home.

WHISKEY

Distilled from malted grains, whiskey has a multitude of varieties. Each style differs from the last, from sweeter American whiskey aged in brand-new barrels to smokier and peatier Scotch and Irish whiskeys. The latter two varieties inherit some of their character from the used wine or whiskey barrels that they are aged in.

LIQUEURS

A liqueur is a sweetened distilled spirit, flavored with fruit, herbs, spices, and more. Generally lower in alcohol than a spirit, liqueurs are used widely in cocktails, adding layers of flavor that a base spirit cannot provide.

ABSINTHE

Folklore and mythology gloss many a tale of the history of absinthe. Banned in many countries at the start of the twentieth century because of its perceived hallucinogenic qualities and formerly a favorite tipple of the bohemian art scene of that time, absinthe was legalized again only very recently. Its reputation remains, but has unfortunately been diluted by unscrupulous producers who have been known to dye the product green as opposed to infusing the final distilled spirit with the eponymous *Artemisia absinthium,* commonly known as wormwood. As with many aniseed-flavored drinks, using water in dilution can create a beautiful cloudy (louche) effect and sometimes give an unusual pearlescence to the final drink.

BITTERS

Bitters are an alcoholic infusion used to "season" drinks—the salt and pepper of the cocktail world, if you will. Commonly made using herbs, spices, and citrus peel, they tend to be bitter in flavor and require just a few drops to modify a drink. Bitters can be omitted or substituted with other flavors in the recipes that follow, but we think it is worth starting off your home bar with a couple of varieties. You can taste your drinks before and after the addition of bitters if you are unsure about investing in furthering the range in your pantry.

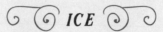

Ice is one of, if not the most important ingredients in any cocktail and the most frequently found ingredient across the whole genre. Ice to a bartender is what fire is to a chef. Chilling the drink is not the only reason that ice is ubiquitous; dilution of the drink is also a very important part of creating palatable flavors. Once the ice melts, it becomes a part of the drink and not just the chilling agent; the right amount of dilution is important, as it helps create a smooth, well-balanced drink. Too little dilution can lead to a cocktail tasting harsh, where the base spirit overpowers all other flavors. Alternatively, an over-diluted drink can taste watery and bland. Therefore, it is always important to taste the drink after shaking and ensure it is perfectly balanced before you strain it into the glass.

CRUSHED ICE

Crushed ice can be bought readily from ice suppliers or obtained from your local friendly bartender. The best method of home production we have found, though, is to use a food-safe hessian (jute) sack and a mallet! Fill the bag, place on a chopping board, hold tight, and release some stress by bashing up the ice!

ICE SPEARS

Whereas a stack of ice cubes would obviously do the trick here, a molded spear of ice definitely adds more of a wow factor to your highball drink, especially if the ice is frozen with a garnish inside—think Bloody Mary with a thin stick of celery, leaves and all frozen inside, or a cucumber wedge frozen in ice used like a swizzle stick in our Cucumber Frames cocktail (page 52). Silicone spear molds are now readily available in many supermarkets and online.

ICE SPHERES

These are great for use with neat spirits or high-strength cocktails such as the Negroni or Old Fashioned. These look amazing when snugly fitted into a rocks glass and add an element of fun to the drinking process—the ball gently rolls and spins as one sips the drink, slowly diluting along the way. Fill a sphere-shaped mold with water and place inside your freezer for simple ice spheres!

SMALL CUBES

Found in the home, made in an ice cube tray, or bought by the bag, small cubes should be used for shaking and stirring and are perfect for the cocktail beginner to use in most processes.

TECHNIQUES

In this next section, a simplified guide to the various processes used in the making of our drinks.

SHAKING

Shaking is the most commonly recognized cocktail-making technique. In the cocktail recipes that follow in Part II, we will describe how much and how hard you need to shake to get the desired result. We prefer to use a Boston glass and shaker tin, but there are other varieties of shaker that will do the job just as well. Build your cocktail in the glass part, over ice, if using, then place the steel tin over the top, tapping it firmly to create a seal. Tip it upside down so that the glass faces up, then shake over your shoulder. When the metal part frosts, your drink has been chilled. To separate, hold the glass part facing up, and tap where the two parts meet with the heel of your hand. This can be tricky to get the hang of, so first practice with empty vessels or with water and ice so as not to risk losing precious stock!

DRY SHAKING

Dry shaking means shaking a drink without ice. This technique is generally used with dairy ingredients or egg whites, or when we want to add air to or "fluff" a drink without too much dilution. It is generally followed by a "wet shake," with ice, to chill and dilute the drink.

REVERSE DRY SHAKING

A technique we favor in this book is the reverse of the above process. Here the wet shake comes first, allowing the foam created by the subsequent dry shake to remain, as opposed to the traditional order, where foam created in the dry shake can be lost by then shaking with ice.

STRAINING AND DOUBLE STRAINING

Usually the step that follows shaking, straining removes ice from the drink before pouring the final drink. Some recipes call for the whole thing to be "dumped" into the final receptacle, but most will require the drink to be strained over fresh ice, or even double (fine) strained (using a second fine strainer, tea strainer, or sieve) to remove the tiniest broken fragments of ice, which can affect the final aesthetic, dilution, flavor, and mouthfeel (texture) of a drink.

BUILDING

The simplest of all the processes, building begins with filling your cocktail glass with ice, then pouring over the ingredients in the order listed.

LAYERING/FLOATING

Layering is used to create an impressive visual effect. Simply pour liquid components of different weights or viscosities gently over the back of a spoon, in order of weight, with the heaviest first, to create layers in the final drink. This term is sometimes used for when a product is added after the main component of the drink has been poured.

STIRRING

Using a mixing glass and upended barspoon adds a touch of elegance to this process, but the home bartender is quite within their rights to use any type of spoon/chopstick or glass/jar/pitcher that suits the volumes of liquid required. The size of ice cube will influence the dilution rate here, so be sure to keep tasting to achieve the desired effect.

INFUSION, MACERATION, AND FILTRATION

Infusing a spirit simply involves immersing your chosen flavor, in solid form, in alcohol, allowing the flavors to slowly leach out into the liquid. Herbs, spices, fruits, vegetables, and sweeteners can all work well as infusions.

Macerating is similar to infusing but is used for hardier solids and involves breaking up the solid to increase the surface area and speed the infusion process. The application of gentle heat will speed the process, too, but it's important not to let the ingredients get too hot—think airing cupboard or a warm windowsill in the summer.

Be careful to taste your infusions frequently; stronger flavors and softer fruits will infuse faster than lighter flavors and hardier botanicals, such as nuts and dried herbs, and spices will take a lot longer. Tea and coffee will infuse (or cold brew) very quickly and be ready in a matter of hours.

After you infuse or macerate a liquid you will most likely need to filter out some solid residue. The method of filtration depends on the flavoring agents used. Nuts, tea, coffee beans, and hard/dried spices can easily be removed using a fine strainer or sieve. Soft fruits and vegetables may need to be strained using a coffee filter or muslin cloth. Beware, though—using fabric or paper will result in some loss of precious fluid!

FAT WASHING

While this may sound like an activity performed by a specialized laundromat, it is actually a technique used to imbue the flavor of almost anything into a spirit by first infusing the flavor into a fat, then stirring the fat into the alcohol, then removing the fat by chilling and straining the mixture. This technique is thought to have been borrowed from perfumers, who have long used a version of fat washing (known as solvent extraction) to extract aromas from certain compounds.

We found that in some cases, fat washing was the perfect way to recreate some of the fantastical flavors described by Carroll in the Alice books, when the desired flavors were too unique to have been commercially produced.

One of the wonderful results of this process is that not only can we replicate a certain flavor very easily within a drink, but also the texture of the liquid is altered slightly by the miniscule particles of flavored fats left behind in the liquid after chilling and straining, giving the drink a much smoother mouthfeel.

GARNISHING TECHNIQUES

A great cocktail is made up of more than just the taste; the aroma, glassware, and garnish are also important components. The right garnish can help elevate the entire drink, making the cocktail a far more enjoyable occasion. In this section we explain the techniques used to create a range of traditional garnishes.

RIMMING

Rimming is a popular way to garnish a glass, commonly using salt or sugar. After using a piece of citrus fruit to carefully wet the rim of the glass, dip the rim in a saucer filled with your dried, powdered garnish, so that it sticks to the rim of the glass. Holding the glass upside down, gently tap off any excess from the glass with your knuckle, then wipe the inside of the rim with a dry tissue or cloth to remove any particles that may taint the actual drink before pouring and serving.

CITRUS TWISTS

A prettier and more elegant alternative than simply dropping a slice of citrus into the drink, twists are easily created by cutting a long, wide strip of zest from the fruit with a sharp knife or peeler. Flip the peel over and scrape off the bitter white pith, trim to a neat shape with a paring knife, then roll it around a barspoon, straw, or chopstick to curl. Performing this last stage over the top of your drink will impart some precious citrus oils into the beverage, adding a layer to the flavor and aroma.

DEHYDRATING

Dehydrating is a method of removing moisture from food to preserve it. By dehydrating fruit en masse, you can have a pantry supply of ready-to-go garnishes that will last for a month or more in a jar or sealed container. You can float them on top of your cocktails, nibble them as snacks, or hang them on your Christmas tree!

Equipment and Tools

In terms of tools, a professional bartender's arsenal is never complete. There will always be a cool new product on the market that we want, that we convince ourselves will be a lifesaver. Although these tools can produce great results, much like that kitchen gadget you got for your birthday (vegetable spiralizer, anyone?), there is almost certainly a way to get similar results without it. These pieces of apparatus add layers to the theater of bartending found in cocktail bars, but tasty drinks can easily be whipped up at home using jam jars and dessert spoons! Most tools required for our drinks can be found in a relatively well-stocked home kitchen, but here follows a short list of items we recommend you seek out.

BARSPOON

The variety that we prefer is a long-handled spoon, decorated with a screw thread and with a flat disk on the end. This disk can be used to assist in floating/ layering (liquid is poured, through a speed pourer, down the spoon's screw thread, like a spiral slide) onto the top of another, heavier fluid. A barspoon is mainly used for stirring a drink in a mixing glass.

MIXING GLASS

In no way does this need to be fancy or ornate for the home bartender. The only requirements are that the glass is large enough to mix several drinks (with ice, so 16 ounces [470 ml] or more) and has a pouring spout (otherwise we would recommend a large pickle jar!).

JIGGER/MEASURE

This could be an egg cup or a shot glass in times of need, but a jigger is relatively cheap to buy, so treat yourself. Our favorite kind is the double-ended 1-ounce/2-ounce (30-ml/60-ml) jigger. It is conical at each end and looks like an egg timer shape. Some can be found with graded smaller measures engraved on the inside of the jigger.

COCKTAIL SHAKER

Again, multiple varieties of these are available. We like the Boston shaker. This comes in two pieces, one tapered stainless-steel tin, and another smaller piece of the same shape, usually made from glass but also sometimes stainless steel.

SPEED POURERS

Rubber and steel pouring spouts are not essential but really help with accurate measuring, especially when it comes to using some of the smaller measures. These fit snugly in the neck of a standard bottle and can be bought with matching covers, which prevent evaporation and contamination from dust and fruit flies. Colloquially known as nipples (e.g., "Brian, where's that bag of nipples?") these are worth the small outlay to protect your valuable stock.

HAND JUICER (MEXICAN ELBOW)

Again, not crucial for the home bartender, but the more drinks you make, the more useful you will find this tool. It helps yield more juice than squeezing by hand or using a traditional tabletop juicer and bowl. It's inexpensive and easy to find online, or in any good kitchen supply shop.

HAWTHORNE (SPRING) STRAINER

This device sits on the top of the cocktail shaker and separates ice from liquid. Hawthorne is the market leader in this field.

FINE STRAINER

Sometimes sold as a tea strainer, this is a small sieve to filter any tiny particles or shards of ice that are not caught by your spring strainer.

ADDITIONAL HOME BAR EQUIPMENT

Cutting board

Paring knife

Corkscrew

Fruit/vegetable peeler

Fine grater

Funnel

Mason jars

GLASSWARE

As with the kitchen equipment, most households will have a small range of glassware, some of which will be suitable for cocktail service. There are a multitude of different glassware shapes and styles on the market, including Collins, highball, rocks, martini, coupe, hurricane, margarita, flute, goblet, and more. We aim to limit the amount of glassware required for you to make the full range of drinks displayed within these pages. A few well-selected types can be used to curate a range to suit all purposes.

HIGHBALL

As the name suggests, this is a tall glass, and for all intents and purposes, the same as a Collins glass (which takes its name from the Tom/John Collins cocktails, served long), available in a few different sizes, from 8 ounces (240 ml) up to 14 ounces (410 ml). We find the 12-ounce (360-ml) size to be the best to cover all bases. Used to serve long drinks, or spirits with a mixer or beer.

ROCKS

Similar in shape to the slightly larger old-fashioned glass, this short tumbler is used to serve neat spirits (or on the rocks, with ice) and short cocktails, such as the Old Fashioned or Negroni. The average size is 6 to 8 ounces (180 to 240 ml), with double rocks/ old-fashioned holding 12 to 14 ounces (360 to 410 ml). We favor a rocks glass with a hefty base: it just feels right in your hand and prevents some warming of the drink inside when held and swirled around by the drinker.

COUPE

Pronounced *coop,* as opposed to *coopay,* this glass is also known as a champagne coupe or champagne saucer. This wide, shallow, bowl-shaped, stemmed vessel is notoriously difficult to carry across a busy bar when full but carries an air of elegance that the more popular, cone-shaped, stemmed martini (or cocktail) glass cannot give. Find one that holds around 5 ounces (150 ml) for optimum results.

NICK AND NORA

This goblet-style glass is named after Nick and Nora Charles, a fictional detective duo with a penchant for cocktails. A conical bowl atop an ornate stem, it is a great alternative to a coupe or martini glass and is designed to hold a slightly smaller cocktail, usually 3 to 4 ounces (90 to 120 ml).

FLUTE

A tall, stemmed wineglass, a flute was originally used for serving Champagne. It is the ultimate in perceived elegance. The recent growth of prosecco and other "everyday" sparkling wines means that tables strewn with flutes are likely to be found in popular bars around the globe.

In addition to these types of glasses, some of our drinks can be served in teapots, with cups and saucers, at your inevitable Mad Hatter's Tea Party, and others in tiny apothecary-style "Drink Me" bottles. Some people like to use jam jars topped with gingham cloth and pierced with a straw. Whatever you choose, find a suitable-size receptacle that suits your style, then experiment and have fun with these recipes.

PART II

COCKTAILS

OFF WITH HER HEAD

"The Queen had only one way of settling all difficulties, great or small."

The Queen of Hearts has a penchant for dispensing executions at will, but it is not until the final act, after Alice has given her evidence, that the Queen's scorn turns on our protagonist and she screams her sentence in her customary manner: *"Off with her head!"* In the perfect nonsensical nature of Wonderland and its twisted interpretation of time, we wanted to start this book with a drink inspired by the very end of *Alice's Adventures in Wonderland*. This drink has a thick head, which, when drunk, will be cut through by the smoky profile of the mezcal and the sweetness of the raisin.

YIELD

1 cocktail

INGREDIENTS

1.5 oz (45 ml) Quiquiriqui Matatlan mezcal

1 oz (30 ml) fresh squeezed lime juice

1 oz (30 ml) raisin and apple syrup (page 94)

4 drops and 1 long dash Bob's Lavender Bitters

1 egg white

1 edible flower

METHOD

1. Start by filling a Boston glass with cubed ice, then pour over the mezcal, lime juice, syrup and 4 drops of the bitters. Add the egg white to the glass. **2.** Assemble the shaker and give the mixture a very hard shake for 8 to 10 seconds. Try and be forceful, as this will help the egg white form a thick foam. **3.** Fine strain the mixture into a fresh clean Boston shaker and dry shake (shake without ice) for a further 8 to 10 seconds. Fine strain the mixture into your coupe glass; the foam should rise and settle into a thick head. **4.** Garnish with an edible flower on top of the foam and a long dash of lavender bitters.

THE GOLDEN AFTERNOON

"All in the golden afternoon,
Full leisurely we glide,
For both our oars, with little skill,
By little arms are plied."

This poem is the precursor to all of Alice's adventures in Wonderland and sets the scene for everything to come. It is a beautiful start to the novel and we wanted to create an equally beautiful drink for you to begin your adventure into the array of cocktails Wonderland has to offer. This refreshing cooler is the perfect way to bridge the gap between afternoon and evening, an alcoholic twist on the Arnold Palmer, and proof that simplicity can yield great results.

1 cocktail

INGREDIENTS

½ lemon

1.5 oz (45 ml) Bulleit bourbon whiskey

1.5 oz (45 ml) iced tea mix (page 123)

1.5 oz (45 ml) ginger ale

1 sprig fresh mint

METHOD

1. Make a lemon twist before cutting your lemon for juicing, then fill a highball glass with fresh ice cubes and pour the bourbon over the ice, adding the juice of half a lemon and the iced tea. Use a barspoon to agitate the liquids, then top with the ginger ale. **2.** Garnish with a substantial mint sprig, slapped in between your palms to release the aroma, then add the lemon twist you prepared earlier, curling it over the drink to release the fragrant oils.

Note: This recipe can be easily scaled up to make a pitcher when you have guests. Simply ice and garnish your glasses before pouring from the jug, using your barspoon to control how much additional ice is added from the pitcher. Top the glasses with the ginger ale individually to retain some fizz!

WHITE RABBIT

"Oh dear! Oh dear! I shall be too late!"

T he most memorable of Lewis Carroll's creations, the White Rabbit is the creature who entices Alice to enter Wonderland and is a central figure in this imaginative world. Any collection of cocktails from Wonderland would be remiss for not including a drink inspired by the time-conscious critter. This drink has a thick, creamy texture and a well-balanced taste that blends the vanilla sweetness of the buttercream with the tart of the gooseberry and a touch of floral elderflower, while its crisp white color is perfectly reminiscent of our furry friend.

— YIELD —

1 cocktail

INGREDIENTS

1 piece all-butter shortbread biscuit, finely crumbled

1 teaspoon unsalted butter

1 oz (30 ml) vanilla bean and
cake frosting–infused vodka (page 128)

1 oz (30 ml) half-and-half

2 barspoons gooseberry jam

0.5 oz (15 ml) Briottet Fleur de Sureau
(elderflower) liqueur

0.5 oz (15 ml) fresh squeezed lemon juice

¼ teaspoon roasted lemon zest (page 137)

1 dehydrated lemon wheel (page 136)

 METHOD

1. Crumble the shortbread biscuit into fine crumbs on a small plate, wipe the outside rim of a coupe glass with the butter until there is an even coating, then sprinkle the shortbread dust over the outside of the inverted glass, allowing the dust to stick to the butter and create a biscuit rim. **2.** Place all the liquid ingredients into a Boston glass and dry shake to allow the gooseberry jam to break down and become a part of the drink. Then add cubed ice to the mixture, close the shaker on top of the glass, and give it a long, hard shake before straining the cocktail into your glass. **3.** Sprinkle a little roasted lemon zest over the surface of the finished drink; this sharpness will contrast with the buttery shortbread rim beautifully. Garnish with the dehydrated lemon wheel.

DRINK ME

"It had, in fact, a sort of mixed flavor of cherry-tart, custard, pine-apple, roast turkey, toffee, and hot buttered toast."

The quintessential drink of Wonderland, this potion's magical properties contort Alice's body and set her up to start her adventures into Wonderland. With this drink we wanted to create a curious cocktail that dared to blend the wide array of flavors Lewis Carroll references in his novel. The complex flavors of the turkey- and toast-infused rums balance out with the sweetness of the cherry liqueur to create an enjoyable drink with distinct taste that will live long in the memory. This is the perfect drink for a party, as it involves an element of theater and allows you to pre-batch and bottle the drink in advance.

YIELD

1 cocktail

INGREDIENTS

0.5 oz (15 ml) Cherry Heering

0.5 oz (15 ml) vanilla bean and cake frosting–infused vodka (page 128)

0.5 oz (15 ml) buttered toast–infused rum (page 125)

0.5 oz (15 ml) turkey rum (page 132)

1 oz (30 ml) pineapple juice

0.25 oz (7 ml) toffee syrup

0.25 oz (7 ml) fresh squeezed lemon juice

METHOD

1. Add all the ingredients to a Boston glass over cubed ice, give the mixture a hard shake, then use a funnel to fine strain the mixture into a 5-ounce (140-ml) glass bottle.

2. Cork the bottle and garnish with a brown paper tag labeled "Drink Me." Serve the bottle alongside a Nick and Nora glass, allowing your guests to pour the drink out themselves. Be sure to keep any batched bottles chilled. You will need to buy a runny toffee syrup for this drink; if the syrup is too thick, you may need to implement a dry shake (see page 20 at the start of the process.)

POOL OF TEARS

"She was in the pool of tears which she had wept when she was nine feet high."

*T*he Pool of Tears is one of Alice's early encounters with the strange happenings in Wonderland. After eating the "Eat Me" cake, her body starts to stretch and grow at a supernatural rate. Alice's understandable reaction is to break down and cry, yet the tears she lets out simply fill the room and form a pool of water that carries Alice further into her adventure. Alice floating in a pool of tears is an image which resonates with readers and is a powerful, early scene that we wanted to reference when designing this book. We wanted to create a drink as salty as a gulp of Alice's tears. In this drink we balance our homemade rosemary and salt syrup with the sweetness of the pear juice and complex profile of the calvados to create a sharp, refreshing drink.

YIELD

1 cocktail

INGREDIENTS

1 lemon slice (to rim)

1 teaspoon sea salt

1.5 oz (45 ml) Calvados

1 oz (30 ml) pear juice

0.5 oz (15 ml) Briottet Poire William (pear) liqueur

0.5 oz (15 ml) rosemary and salt syrup (page 93)

0.5 oz (15 ml) fresh squeezed lemon juice

1 sprig rosemary

METHOD

1. First, chill your coupe glass with ice until it is frosted, then discard the ice and rim the lip of the glass with the lemon, then dust with the salt, ensuring an even layer of salt sticks to the outer rim of the glass. 2. Fill a Boston glass with fresh, cubed ice. 3. Next add the liquid ingredients to the Boston glass and shake for roughly 10 seconds before fine straining the mixture into the glass. 4. Flame a sprig of rosemary over a gas flame on your stovetop or with a lighter and place it across the rim of the glass, allowing the aromas to wash over you as you sip your drink.

CURIOUSER AND CURAÇAO

"'Curiouser and curiouser!' cried Alice."

Our protagonist becomes quite anxious about the inexplicable physical changes the "Drink Me" bottle and "Eat Me" cake have bestowed upon her. If ever you needed a drink to steady your nerves it might be after finding yourself in Wonderland, and this drink is the perfect tonic for such a situation. Built around the Caribbean orange liqueur Curaçao, it is a contemporary twist on a classic Old Fashioned.

As its name suggests, the Old Fashioned has some history. It dates to the 1880s and to this day remains a stalwart of the modern cocktail menu. This twist uses caramelized fruit to add the sweet aspect of the drink and makes for a beautifully balanced alternative to many a bartender's perennial favorite. Classic Old Fashioned recipes call for many minutes of stirring, so that the sugar will dissolve, but because this recipe uses a fruit puree and orange liqueur instead of cubed sugar, the need for stirring is greatly reduced, and helps simply to dilute the drink to taste.

— YIELD —
1 cocktail

INGREDIENTS

2 barspoons burnt peach puree (page 120)

1.5 oz (45 ml) Bulleit bourbon whiskey

0.75 oz (23 ml) orange Curaçao (page 110)

3 drops Bob's orange and mandarin bitters

1 burnt peach slice (page 120)

¼ teaspoon grated nutmeg

METHOD

1. Add fresh cubed ice to a mixing glass or Boston glass, pour the burnt peach puree through a fine strainer over the ice, and use the end of your barspoon to help the liquid through the mesh of your strainer. **2.** Add the bourbon, Orange Curaçao and bitters next, stirring gently for at least a minute, tasting for the desired level of dilution. **3.** Strain the cocktail into your heftiest rocks glass over a large ice sphere (or fresh ice cubes). Garnish the drink with a burnt peach slice dusted with grated nutmeg.

THE CAUCUS CHASER

"Everybody has won,
and all must have prizes."

T he Caucus Race is an absurd race with no start, finish, winner, or loser, another of the many weird and whimsical endeavors Alice encounters in Wonderland. When the race is run, and the dodo has called the proceedings to an end, all competitors are declared winners. We designed the Caucus Chaser to be the perfect prize to all competitors in your very own caucus race. The perfect follow-up to any bout of physical exertion, it is a refreshing, low-alcohol drink that makes it the perfect midafternoon sharpener.

1 cocktail

INGREDIENTS

1 oz (30 ml) Bramley & Gage (plum) liqueur

1 oz (30 ml) orange Curaçao (page 110)

1 oz (30 ml) Briottet Crème de Châtaigne
(chestnut) liqueur

0.5 oz (15 ml) fresh squeezed lemon juice

1 egg white

1 barspoon plum jam

1 teaspoon roasted orange zest (page 137)

METHOD

1. Pour the Bramley & Gage, Curaçao, and chestnut liqueur over ice into a Boston glass, then add the lemon juice and shake for 6 to 8 seconds. **2.** Fine strain out the ice and any rogue lemon seeds, add the egg white and plum jam to the Boston glass, then dry shake (without ice) for a further 6 to 8 seconds. **3.** Fine strain the thickened cocktail into a coupe, garnish with a sprinkle of roasted orange zest, and drink immediately—the perfect preparation for a caucus race.

DIGGING FOR APPLES

"I'm here! Digging for apples, yer honour!"

Pat is one of the White Rabbit's servants and we soon learn that his favorite pastime is as quaint as they come: digging for apples. This delightful hobby fueled us to create a drink that Pat would enjoy more so than any other inhabitant of Wonderland, a drink that blends the strong apple flavors of Calvados with the rich Gala apple puree. This cocktail brings together some classic British flavors you would expect to find in a world created by Lewis Carroll: vanilla, cinnamon, and apple combine to make a warming drink with a very familiar taste.

YIELD
1 cocktail

INGREDIENTS

1 oz (30 ml) Calvados

0.5 oz (15 ml) Briottet Crème de Noisette (hazelnut) liqueur

2 oz (60 ml) apple puree (page 121)

0.5 oz (15 ml) spiced cinnamon syrup (page 100)

1 oz (30 ml) whipping cream

2 teaspoons vanilla bean and
cake frosting–infused vodka (page 128)

¼ teaspoon ground cinnamon

METHOD

1. Begin by half-filling a Boston glass with ice, then add the Calvados, hazelnut liqueur, apple puree, and cinnamon syrup. Assemble the shaker and give it a medium shake for roughly 8 seconds before fine straining the liquid into a coupe glass. **2.** Next, using a clean Boston glass and shaker, add the cream and vanilla vodka and give it all a very hard shake (dry shake) for 10 to 15 seconds. This will aerate or thicken the cream mixture, making it light enough to float on top of the drink. **3.** You now want to layer the cream mixture on top of the cocktail base. To do this, strain the vodka cream into a small jug. Holding the tip of your barspoon on top of the surface of the cocktail, lightly touching the surface of the drink, pour the cream very slowly from the jug onto the back of the spoon, and it should settle distinctly on top of the drink. **4.** Garnish by sprinkling a little ground cinnamon over the top, so that it decorates the white surface of the cocktail and lends a familiar apple pie aroma to the party.

CUCUMBER FRAMES

"It was just possible it had fallen into a cucumber-frame, or something of the sort."

At the start of the fourth chapter, Alice drinks from an unlabeled bottle and quickly starts to grow; so quickly in fact that she soon finds herself trapped within the confines of the White Rabbit's house, just as he is trying to enter. Waves of Alice's enormous hands are met by small shrieks and the sound of breaking glass, and she wonders at the number of cucumber frames being trampled. We took this tragic waste of perfectly good cucumbers as inspiration when deciding to incorporate the staple salad ingredient into a cocktail, creating a refreshing drink with a distinct flavor. The drink blends herbal flavors with the fresh cucumber while utilizing sake, a drastically underused cocktail ingredient.

1 cocktail

INGREDIENTS

2 oz (60 ml) cucumber vodka (page 116)

2 oz (60 ml) sake

2 oz (60 ml) dry vermouth (page 114)

3 drops Bob's Coriander Bitters

1 sprig cilantro

1 cucumber spear

METHOD

1. Add the vodka, sake, dry vermouth, and bitters to an iced Boston glass. Shake well and strain over fresh ice into a highball glass. **2.** Finish by garnishing with a healthy sprig of cilantro, slapped in your palms to release the aromas, and a long spear of cucumber, to be used like a swizzle stick to play with your cocktail and nibble on at will.

THE CATERPILLAR'S HOOKAH

*"a large blue caterpillar . . .
quietly smoking a long hookah"*

The Blue Caterpillar is a languid and sleepy creature whose laid-back, yet cryptic nature we've replicated in this cocktail. The Scotch has a smoky profile that blends perfectly with the lemon and sage syrup to create a complex yet easily drinkable tipple, while the burning sage adds some theater and is the perfect reflection of the caterpillar's smoking hookah.

YIELD

1 cocktail

INGREDIENTS

1.5 oz (45 ml) Talisker 10-year
single malt Scotch whisky
1 oz (30 ml) fino sherry
1 oz (30 ml) lemon and sage syrup (page 98)
2 fresh sage leaves
1 crispy sage garnish (page 138)

METHOD

1. Add the Scotch whisky, sherry, and syrup to a mixing glass with ice and stir well for 2 to 3 minutes. **2.** Next, place the sage leaves onto a wooden block, light them with a match, wait for them to catch fire fully, hold an inverted rocks glass over the burning leaves for a couple of seconds, then place the glass over the leaves, trapping the smoke inside. Allow the glass to fill with smoke. **3.** When it is well smoked, turn it the right way up, add fresh cubed ice, and strain your cocktail from the mixing glass over the ice. **4.** Garnish with a crispy sage leaf. This drink is best served immediately to fully enjoy the aromas.

THE MUSHROOM

"One side will make you grow taller, and the other side will make you grow shorter."

When Alice eats the mushroom, her body is manipulated by its magical qualities, shrinking to a minute size before her neck grows so long that her head is poking up out of the trees. The qualities the mushroom possesses are both confusing and alien to Alice, for many years, absinthe was believed to have similar mind-bending features. It is a complex spirit, with a wide variety of flavor profiles, but always be wary of what you are buying and ensure it is "real absinthe," not the vile, dyed green vodka sometimes passed off as absinthe. Alcohol affects the human body in a wide variety of ways across its different forms; with absinthe it results in a mild sensation of lightheadedness, which makes it the perfect spirit to replicate the transformative and hallucinogenic properties of the mushroom.

YIELD

1 cocktail

INGREDIENTS

0.5 oz (15 ml) real absinthe

1 oz (30 ml) Cocchi Americano

1 oz (30 ml) Briottet Rose Liqueur

Edible dehydrated rose petals

METHOD

1. Add ice to a mixing glass to fill halfway, top with the absinthe, Cocchi Americano, and Briottet Rose Liqueur, then stir until the ice has half melted, roughly 1 minute.

2. Use a hawthorne strainer to strain the liquid into a Nick and Nora glass and garnish with a sprinkling of dehydrated rose petals.

Note: Dehydrated rose petals are readily available online; alternatively, if you have a dehydrator you can easily prepare them at home (see page 25). Take care to dehydrate only edible flower petals—if in doubt, do not consume!

PIG AND PEPPER

"I speak severely to my boy,
I beat him when he sneezes;
For he can thoroughly enjoy
The pepper when he pleases!"

The Pig and Pepper chapter is full of oddities, from the strong pepper flavor lingering in the air to Alice mistaking a piglet for a baby child. This idea of mistaken identities and hidden flavors helped inspire us to create a short drink that on the surface appears to be a standard Bloody Mary shot, but has been infused with unexpected meaty flavors of smoky pancetta and spicy pink peppercorns.

YIELD

1 cocktail

INGREDIENTS

1 slice crispy pancetta

1 oz (30 ml) pancetta and pink peppercorn vodka (page 130)

1 oz (30 ml) Bloody Mary mix (page 122)

METHOD

1. Pan-fry a thin slice of pancetta in a dry skillet over medium heat until crispy and charred. Reserve. **2.** Pour the vodka and Bloody Mary mix into a mixing glass with an ice cube, stir to chill, then strain into a 2-ounce (60-ml) shot glass. **3.** Lay the slice of pancetta on top of the glass as a garnish, using a cocktail stick to help it sit on the rim if required.

THE DUCHESS'S SOUP

" 'There's certainly too much pepper in that soup!' Alice said to herself."

When Alice first meets the Duchess, she is sitting down stroking a baby pig while the cook stirs a cauldron of soup, wafting a strong scent of pepper into the air, so much pepper that it sets Alice off into a sneezing fit. Such a powerfully seasoned soup sounded like an abrasive and intriguing flavor to us and we decided that this most common of spices would be the perfect flavor to incorporate into a cocktail. This drink pairs the spice of the cracked black pepper syrup with the subtle sweetness of fresh strawberry to create a palatable take on the Duchess's soup.

— YIELD —

1 cocktail

INGREDIENTS

1 lemon wedge
1 teaspoon fresh cracked black pepper

1 large strawberry

1 oz (30 ml) Half Hitch gin

0.5 oz (15 ml) cracked black pepper syrup (page 106)

0.5 oz (15 ml) fresh squeezed lemon juice

1.75 oz (52 ml) sparkling wine

1 dehydrated strawberry garnish (see page 25)

METHOD

1. Start by rimming your coupe first with the lemon wedge and then the freshly cracked black pepper, ensuring an even layer of pepper sticks to the outer rim of the glass. **2.** Next, dice and muddle the strawberry in a Boston glass, ensure the fruit is well worked and all the juice has been released, then add the gin, cracked black pepper syrup, and lemon juice and give the mixture a hard, dry shake (no ice) for roughly 5 seconds. **3.** Fine strain the mixture into a fresh, clean Boston glass, ensuring you strain out any leftover fruit pulp, squeezing the liquid through the strainer with your barspoon. Add fresh cubed ice to the clean Boston glass and shake the mixture again for a further 5 seconds. **4.** Fine strain the liquid into the prepared coupe and top with sparkling wine, leaving a finger-width gap from the lip of the glass. **5.** Finish the drink by floating a dehydrated slice of strawberry on the drink's surface.

CUP OF MAD TEA

"It's always tea-time, and we've no time to wash the things between whiles."

No collection of cocktails from Wonderland would be complete without including a Mad Tea, a drink that keeps the March Hare, Mad Hatter, and Dormouse suitably lubricated as they enjoy their perpetual tea party. Our version consists of Assam and Darjeeling infusions to create a malty alcoholic brew, while the dash of absinthe adds an extra touch of madness to the drink.

INGREDIENTS

1.5 oz (45 ml) Darjeeling gin (page 118)

1 oz (30 ml) Assam tea syrup (page 103)

1 oz (30 ml) blood orange juice

1 teaspoon real absinthe

1 dehydrated blood orange wheel (page 136)

METHOD

1. Add the gin, syrup, blood orange juice, and absinthe to a mixing glass over cubed ice. Stir the mixture for 1½ minutes, or until the liquid has roughly doubled in volume. **2.** Fine strain the mixture into an ornate teacup and garnish with a slice of dehydrated blood orange.

PAINTING THE ROSES RED

*"Would you tell me . . .
why you are painting those roses?"*

E lements of comedy and beauty go together in
Wonderland, and the image of a group of cards
painting rose petals red, as they mistakenly
planted a white rose bush instead of red, is the perfect
case in point. The splash of rosewater in this drink creates a flavor in keeping with such an endeavor, and its
bright red color means it should please the Queen and
her very specific expectations.

1 cocktail

INGREDIENTS

1.5 oz (45 ml) Tanqueray London gin

0.5 oz (15 ml) Briottet Crème de Framboise
(raspberry) liqueur

1 oz (30 ml) raspberry and licorice syrup
(page 96)

1 oz (30 ml) fresh squeezed lemon juice

4 drops rosewater

5 oz (150 ml) soda water

Red and white edible flowers

METHOD

1. Pour the gin, rasberry liqueur, raspberry syrup, lemon juice, and rosewater into a Boston glass over fresh cubed ice. Close the shaker and give it a long, hard shake. **2.** Fill a chilled highball glass with ice and strain the final mixture into the glass. **3.** Finally, top the drink with soda water and garnish with red and white edible flowers.

QUEEN OF HEARTS

*"I heard the queen say only yesterday
you deserved to be beheaded!"*

Sweet enough in appearance, this tipple has a rather sour and bitter finish, reminiscent of a certain Queen of Hearts. Both the tequila and Campari give this drink a strong, bitter flavor and a vibrant red color, while the egg white creates a thick head that acts as a base to layer the raspberry heart on top. In this recipe you will be creating a stencil to make a bold and impressive garnish, so make sure you have adequate amounts of cardboard and a sharp box cutter at hand.

YIELD
1 cocktail

INGREDIENTS
1.5 oz (45 ml) Don Julio Anejo tequila

0.5 oz (15 ml) Campari

0.75 oz (22 ml) Briottet Fleur de Sureau
(elderflower) liqueur

0.5 oz (15 ml) fresh squeezed lime juice

1 egg white
1 teaspoon freeze-dried raspberry powder
1 3-inch (7.5 cm) piece of cordstick (or old Un-Birthday Card)

 **METHOD**

To make the stencil: **1.** Place a coupe glass upside down on a piece of cardboard and draw around the rim of the glass with a pencil so that you have a perfect outline of its circumference, then remove the glass. **2.** Now draw a heart that fits inside the circle rim you have already drawn. **3.** Use a craft knife or box cutter to cut out the heart shape, discard it, and use the cardboard you have left as your stencil.

To make the drink: **1.** Pour the tequila, Campari, and elderflower liqueur into a Boston glass with cubed ice and use a hand press to juice the lime into the mixture. Then shake for 20 seconds and strain out the ice for the next stage, the dry shake. **2.** Add the egg white to the Boston glass and give the mixture a hard shake for roughly 8 seconds, then pour straight into the coupe. The egg white should create a firm layer of foam that settles at the top of the drink.

To finish: **1.** Place the stencil on top of the glass and sift the freeze-dried raspberry powder onto the stencil, making sure the surface is evenly covered with no gaps. Remove the stencil and you should have a perfect heart, a bold and impressive drink fit for a queen.

THE PINK FLAMINGO

*"The balls were live hedgehogs,
the mallets live flamingoes."*

When Alice is invited by the Queen to play croquet she isn't expecting to be handed a live flamingo; it is a playful image steeped in Lewis Carroll's absurdist nature while highlighting how all the creatures of Wonderland bend to the will of the Queen. We wanted to create a drink that matched this spirit while adding an air of sophistication. The vibrant pink color and delicate balance of flavors make this drink something you could quaff down at your very own croquet party.

~ YIELD ~
1 cocktail

⟨ ⟨ INGREDIENTS ⟩ ⟩

1 oz (30 ml) Cîroc vodka

1 oz (30 ml) Briottet Pamplemousse Rose
(pink grapefruit) liqueur

0.5 oz (15 ml) grenadine (page 104)

Juice of ½ grapefruit

3 drops Bob's Orange and Mandarin Bitters

3 to 4 oz (90 to 120 ml) sparkling wine

Small piece dehydrated grapefruit wheel (page 136)

⟨ ⟨ METHOD ⟩ ⟩

1. Fill a Boston shaker with cubed ice and add the vodka, liqueur, grenadine, grapefruit juice, and bitters, giving the mixture a medium-hard shake for 6 to 8 seconds. Fine strain into a large wineglass over fresh ice. 2. Top with the sparkling wine, filling the glass to the brim. 3. Garnish with a small or half wheel of dehydrated grapefruit.

MOCKTURTLETAIL

*"It's the thing Mock Turtle Soup
is made from."*

A drink designed for all young turtles who go to school in the sea to be taught Uglification by a wily old tortoise, this nonalcoholic cocktail combines egg white and soda to a create a frothy texture. It's an elegant and sophisticated take on the mocktail.

YIELD

1 cocktail

INGREDIENTS

1 egg white

1 oz (30 ml) half-and-half

0.5 oz (15 ml) lemon and sage syrup (page 98)

0.5 oz (15 ml) spiced cinnamon syrup (page 100)

1 oz (30 ml) fresh squeezed lemon juice

3 oz (90 ml) soda water

1 teaspoon roasted lemon zest (page 137)

METHOD

1. Chill a rocks glass with some ice cubes. Add the egg white, half-and-half, syrups, and lemon juice to a Boston glass and shake vigorously to emulsify the mixture.

2. Remove the ice from the rocks glass, then pour the mixture from the Boston glass into the rocks glass. Top the drink with soda water so that the drink froths up.

3. Sprinkle some roasted lemon zest in a neat line across the surface of the drink.

LOBSTER QUADRILLE

"You can have no idea what a delightful thing a Lobster Quadrille is!"

This is an odd form of dance introduced to Alice by the Gryphon and the Mock Turtle; you dance along the shoreline and throw lobsters into the sea. It is an absurd and strenuous dance that on completion we feel should be properly rewarded with a fine cocktail. We developed this vibrant pink drink in memory of all those brave lobsters lost to the tide. This drink pairs the bitter flavors from the grapefruit and Campari with the distinctive aniseed taste of pastis and the sweet finish of rhubarb liqueur.

INGREDIENTS

1 oz (30 ml) rhubarb liqueur

0.5 oz (15 ml) Campari

2 oz (60 ml) pink grapefruit juice

4 oz (120 ml) soda water

0.5 oz (15 ml) pastis

1 dehydrated grapefruit wheel (page 136)

METHOD

1. Chill a highball glass with fresh, cubed ice, retaining the ice in the glass. **2.** Fill a Boston glass with cubed ice, then add the rhubarb liqueur, Campari, and grapefruit juice. Shake for 10 to 15 seconds and then strain the mixture into the highball glass. **3.** Top with the soda water, leaving space for a final drizzle of pastis, which gives a beautiful cloudy (louche) effect as the pastis slowly combines with the other ingredients. **4.** Garnish with a dehydrated grapefruit wheel.

THE QUEEN'S TART

"The Knave of Hearts, he stole those tarts,
and took them quite away!"

This is the subject of the court scenes and the Queen's interrogations at the end of the novel— who stole the Queen's tart? It got us thinking that for such a grand inquisition the tart must have had a sumptuous flavor, one that would surely be missed if said tart were stolen or misplaced. With this drink we strove to create a dessert cocktail fit for a queen. The dark chocolate and cherry flavors combine to create the most decadent of tarts.

1 cocktail

INGREDIENTS

Scant 1 oz (28 g) block dark chocolate

1 quality maraschino cherry

1.5 oz (45 ml) Cherry Heering

1.5 oz (45 ml) chocolate cream liqueur

1.5 oz (45 ml) milk

1.5 oz (45 ml) cream

4 drops Bob's Chocolate Bitters

METHOD

1. Start by taking your block of dark chocolate and roughly grate it into flakes. Skewer the cherry with a cocktail stick and, while holding the stick, place the fruit into a bowl of the chocolate flakes and rotate it around until the cherry is fully coated. **2.** Place the cherry on a tray in the refrigerator for 2 hours to set. **3.** Place the Cherry Heering, chocolate liqueur, milk, cream, and chocolate bitters in a Boston glass with some cubed ice. Give the mixture a very hard shake for roughly 8 seconds, or until you have a thick and creamy consistency. **4.** Strain the liquid into a rocks glass over cubed ice and finish with the prepared cherry and an extra sprinkle of dark chocolate flakes.

BEWARE THE JABBERWOCKY

"Beware the Jabberwock, my son!
The jaws that bite, the claws that catch!"

Not to be confused with the traditional Savoy cocktail, the Jabberwock, this cocktail is a new creation inspired solely from the original poem in *Through the Looking-Glass*. The flaming fruit garnish is reminiscent of the Jabberwock "with eyes of flame," and we feel the blend of fig and chestnut flavors paired with the brandy make it a fabulous drink to enjoy while resting by the Tumtum tree, whiffling through a wood, or even galumphing back home.

YIELD

1 cocktail

INGREDIENTS

1.5 oz (45 ml) Rémy Martin Accord Royal Cognac

0.5 oz (15 ml) fig liqueur

0.5 oz (15 ml) chestnut liqueur

½ fresh fig

Demerara sugar

0.25 oz (7 ml) brandy

METHOD

1. Fill a mixing glass with ice cubes, and pour in the cognac and fig and chestnut liqueurs. Stir this mixture with your barspoon for around 1 minute, and move on to the next step. **2.** This simple serve now needs nothing more than an elegant garnish to complete it. Take half a fresh fig, dust the cut side with Demerara sugar, and caramelize it in a nonstick pan with the brandy, tipping the pan so that the warm brandy catches fire—mind your eyebrows! **3.** Place one large ice cube in a Nick and Nora glass and strain the cocktail into it. Your caramelized fig garnish will now sit nicely on top of the ice cube, cooked side up.

THE FRUMIOUS BANDERSNAPS

"Beware the Jubjub bird and shun the frumious Bandersnatch!"

A drink to get your jaw snapping, this one is for cocktail lovers. A strong stiffener, it blends the bitter notes of the Baska Snaps with sweet orange Curaçao to create an effortlessly drinkable short.

YIELD

1 cocktail

INGREDIENTS

1 slice lemon peel

1 oz (30 ml) Baska Snaps Med Malort

1 oz (30 ml) Tanqueray gin

1 oz (30 ml) orange Curaçao (page 110)

METHOD

1. Start by preparing your garnish. Peel off a portion of lemon rind, then use a sharp knife to remove the white pith. **2.** Add the liquid ingredients to a mixing glass over cubed ice and stir for 1 minute, or until the liquid has roughly doubled in volume. **3.** Strain the drink into a rocks glass over fresh ice, rim the glass with the lemon peel, then twist the rind over the glass and drop it in to finish.

BREAD-AND-BUTTERFLY PUDDING

" 'Crawling at your feet,' said the Gnat . . .
'you may observe a Bread-and-Butterfly.' "

The Bread-and-Butterfly is an insect from the fantasy world beyond the looking-glass. It has thin slices of bread and butter for wings and a sugar cube for a head, and survives off a diet of weak tea with cream. This creature is a quintessential creation of Carroll's, personifying familiar British flavors in his characters. Much like Carroll, we enjoy celebrating such sumptuous British flavors, and have created a drink to replicate the traditional dessert, a far more fitting drink for the Bread-and-Butterfly to sustain itself than weak tea.

YIELD

1 cocktail

INGREDIENTS

1.5 oz (45 ml) buttered toast–infused rum (page 125)

0.5 oz (15 ml) fresh squeezed lemon juice

0.5 oz (15 ml) spiced cinnamon syrup (page 100)

0.5 oz (15 ml) raisin and apple syrup (page 94)

1 egg white

Pinch grated nutmeg

Pinch ground cinnamon

METHOD

1. Fill a Boston glass with cubed ice. Add the rum, lemon juice, and syrups. Wet shake and strain out the ice. Then add the egg white and dry shake to create a nice, thick foam. **2.** Pour the mixture into your chosen glass, then dust the concoction with freshly grated nutmeg and ground cinnamon.

DIRTY OYSTER MARTINI

"The eldest Oyster winked his eye,
and shook his heavy head."

This drink was inspired by the poem "The Walrus and the Carpenter" recited by Tweedledum and Tweedledee, a poem in which a whole bed of oysters is gobbled by the eponymous Walrus and Carpenter. As huge oyster fans ourselves, we have long wished for a savory cocktail in which we could enjoy an oyster. A Bloody Mary was the closest we got, until we started to develop a taste for the Dirty Martini, where salty olive brine is used to flavor the drink, along with the traditional olive garnish. Do not be tempted to shake this cocktail, no matter what you may have heard from James Bond or anyone else. Shaking a martini will chill the ingredients a little too much, losing the complexity of your chosen gin and potentially over-diluting the cocktail and leaving you with shards of ice in the final drink.

1 cocktail

INGREDIENTS

1 oyster

0.25 oz (7 ml) Noilly Prat

2 oz (60 ml) Tanqueray gin

Sea salt flakes (optional)

2 green olives, pitted

METHOD

1. Shuck your oyster and reserve, allowing it to rest in a sieve or tea strainer, while collecting the strained liquid beneath. Ours yielded around 0.75 ounce (22 ml) of brine. **2.** Fill a mixing glass with cubed ice. Pour the Noilly Prat and gin over the ice and add the liquor from the oyster, checking carefully for any pieces of grit or shell. Using an upended barspoon, stir the mixture for at least 1 minute. Taste the cocktail. Our 0.75 ounce (23 ml) of oyster brine was just enough for our palates, but some may prefer the drink a little saltier. In this case, a little sprinkle of sea salt flakes should do the trick. **3.** For the garnish, concertina and thread the oyster onto a nice cocktail stick, bookended by a couple of large green olives, then place on the rim of a chilled coupe glass. **4.** Fine strain the cocktail into the coupe and serve.

Un-Birthday Cake Martini

"There are 364 days when you may get un-birthday presents, and only one for birthday presents, you know."

Humpty Dumpty informs Alice of this delightful fact of life in a fantasy world when they meet in *Through the Looking-Glass*. It is an idea we fully support. Never forget to give yourself a daily present, such as this indulgent drink, a fanciful blend of vanilla, cake frosting, and pineapple.

— YIELD —

1 cocktail

INGREDIENTS

¼ oz (7 ml) simple sugar syrup (page 90)

1 teaspoon rainbow sprinkles

1.5 oz (45 ml) vanilla bean and
cake frosting–infused vodka (page 128)

1 oz (30 ml) Briottet Crème de Noisette
(hazelnut) liqueur

0.75 oz (22 ml) Briottet Crème de Framboise
(raspberry) liqueur

0.5 oz (15 ml) fresh squeezed lemon juice

1.5 oz (45 ml) pineapple juice

1 egg white

1 dehydrated lemon wheel (page 136)

METHOD

1. Begin by rimming your chilled martini glass. Pour the simple sugar syrup onto a plate and gently dip the rim into the syrup. **2.** Next, spread the rainbow sprinkles onto a plate and dip the wet rim into it. Set the glass aside. Next, fill a Boston glass to the top with cubed ice. Add the wet ingredients carefully, in the order listed, and shake vigorously to allow the pineapple juice and egg white to thicken the concoction. **3.** Double strain the liquid into the prepared glass, taking care not to disturb the rainbow sprinkle rim. This should mean that you can float a wheel of dehydrated lemon, centered with a short birthday candle. **4.** Finally, dust the drink with more sprinkles and serve. Happy un-birthday!

PART III

BATCH RECIPES

The recipes in this section will help you build a pantry of fabulous homemade ingredients that are used in Part II, but which you can also use to create impressive and indulgent cocktails of your own. The huge benefit of making your own spirits and liqueurs is that you can add flavor profiles to your drinks that aren't commonly available from mainstream brands, while saving yourself money and improving your knowledge and understanding of bartending processes and techniques.

Syrups

The processes for these syrups are very similar, as it is a relatively simple method, but the eventual taste and outcome of the product can vary wildly due to the varying levels of acidity and sweetness in different fruits at different times of the year. The key with these drinks is to trust your taste buds and ensure you have a well-balanced palate. Always remember to taste your syrups (take care when the syrup is hot!) and adjust the quantity of fruit, citrus, or sugar if the result is either too sweet or too tart. Once your syrup has cooled, store in a sealed bottle inside your refrigerator and use within a month.

Simple Sugar Syrup

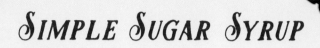

An essential ingredient in every bar, a simple sugar syrup is the perfect way to add sweetness to a drink and balance out the flavor if a cocktail is too bitter or tart. This recipe is quick and easy to make and can easily be scaled up or down in equal quantities.

— YIELD —

14 oz (410 ml)

INGREDIENTS

7 oz (200 g) sugar

7 oz (210 ml) water

METHOD

1. Bring the sugar and water to the boil in a saucepan and simmer until the sugar has dissolved into the water (2 to 3 minutes), stirring constantly. 2. Once the liquid is transparent, remove from heat, leave to cool, and retain in a clean, sealable bottle.

ROSEMARY AND SALT SYRUP

*U*sed in our Pool of Tears (page 44) cocktail, this syrup works well with the fruity apple calvados flavors, but could also be paired with the smoky flavors of a Scotch- or mezcal-based drink. Alternatively, you could mix this spirit with fresh orange juice and soda water to create an exciting soft drink.

— YIELD —

15 oz (440 ml)

INGREDIENTS

7 oz (200 g) sugar

8 oz (240 ml) water

3 sprigs fresh rosemary, washed

2 tablespoons sea salt

METHOD

1. With the sugar and water, make a simple syrup, according to the recipe on page 90. Add 2 of the rosemary sprigs and the sea salt, then bring the pan back to a gentle simmer. 2. Remove the syrup from the heat and allow the flavors to infuse for a couple of hours. 3. Strain the syrup into a clear glass bottle and add the remaining sprig of rosemary directly to the bottle. Label and refrigerate for up to 30 days.

RAISIN AND
APPLE SYRUP

*T*his syrup has a strong and distinctive raisin flavor. We use it in the Off with Her Head and Bread-and-Butterfly Pudding (page 80) drink recipes, but it is equally effective when added to a traditional whisky sour or used to create a unique raisin twist in a margarita.

— YIELD —
20 oz (590 ml)

INGREDIENTS
7 oz (200 g) raisins

9 oz (270 ml) water

5.25 oz (157 ml) apple juice

7 oz (200 g) sugar

METHOD

1. Create a bain-marie by bringing a pan of water to a boil over high heat, then reduce to a simmer; rest a bowl or small pan on top with the base just touching the surface of the water. Fill the empty

pan with the raisins and 9 ounces (270 ml) of the water, then lightly mash the raisins, releasing some of their juice. Allow the raisins to simmer for an hour, or until all the juice has been released.

2. Take the mixture off the heat and strain through a muslin cloth. Add the strained liquid to a clean pan over medium heat along with the apple juice and sugar, and simmer, stirring occasionally, until all the sugar has been fully absorbed. **3.** Remove the syrup from the heat, pour into a sealable container, and let cool.

RASPBERRY AND LICORICE SYRUP

*U*sed in our cocktail Painting the Roses Red (page 64), this syrup has a sweet, fruity profile which would also work perfectly in a range of vodka- or gin-based drinks. Try mixing it with freshly squeezed lemon juice, vodka, and a champagne top to create a refreshing autumnal fizz.

— YIELD —

15 oz (440 ml)

INGREDIENTS

10.75 oz (300 g) raspberries

7 oz (210 ml) water

1.75 oz (50 g) roughly chopped soft,
black licorice candy

5.25 oz (150 g) sugar

METHOD

1. Create a bain-marie by bringing a pan of water to a boil over high heat, then reduce to a simmer; rest a bowl or small pan on top with the base just touching the surface of the water. Fill the empty pan with the raspberries and water, then lightly mash the raspberries, releasing some of their juice. Add the chopped licorice candy and allow the mixture to simmer for an hour, or until all the licorice has fully melted. **2.** Take the mixture off the heat and strain through a muslin cloth. Add the strained liquid to a clean pan over medium heat, add the sugar, and simmer, being careful not to boil and stirring occasionally, until all the sugar has been fully absorbed. **3.** Remove the syrup from the heat, pour into a sealable container, and let cool.

LEMON AND SAGE SYRUP

~~~~~

T his is a tart syrup, with a full and flavorsome blend of herbal and citrus ingredients.We use it to good effect in The Caterpillar's Hookah (page 54), as the sage adds a subtle complementary flavors to the malt whisky. This flavor also works particularly well when used in soft drinks such as the Mockturtletail (page 70); alternatively, you can mix this syrup with fresh lemon juice, soda water, and a sprig of fresh sage to create a thirst-quenching sage lemonade.

YIELD

14 oz (410 ml)

INGREDIENTS

7 oz (210 ml) water

Zest of 3 large lemons

About 1 oz (28 g) sage leaves, roughly chopped

7 oz (200 g) sugar

METHOD

1. Create a bain-marie by bringing a pan of water to a boil over high heat, then reduce to a simmer; rest a bowl or small pan on top with the base just touching

the surface of the water. Add the water to the empty pan. **2.** Roughly chop your lemons, squeeze the juice into the pan, and then add the zest, along with the roughly chopped sage leaves. **3.** Allow the mixture to simmer for an hour, then remove from the heat and strain through a muslin cloth, ensuring all the rinds, seeds, pulp, and sage leaves are removed. **4.** Add the strained liquid to a clean pan over medium heat, add the sugar, and simmer, being careful not to boil and stirring occasionally, until all the sugar has been fully absorbed. **5.** Remove the syrup from the heat, pour into a sealable container, and let cool.

SPICED CINNAMON SYRUP

This syrup is packed full of festive flavors that are perfect for a Christmas fizz or a creamy dessert cocktail. The flavor works best with rich, orange notes like Curaçao, Cointreau, or Triple Sec, or complex apple flavors such as Calvados.

— YIELD —

14 oz (410 ml)

INGREDIENTS

7 oz (210 ml) water

2 cinnamon sticks, roughly chopped

1 tablespoon ground coriander

2 whole cloves

7 oz (200 g) brown sugar

METHOD

1. Create a bain-marie by bringing a pan of water to a boil over high heat, then reduce to a simmer; rest a bowl or small pan on top with the base just touching the surface of the water. Add the water, cinnamon,

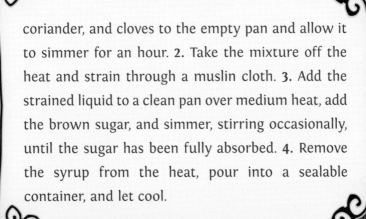

coriander, and cloves to the empty pan and allow it to simmer for an hour. **2.** Take the mixture off the heat and strain through a muslin cloth. **3.** Add the strained liquid to a clean pan over medium heat, add the brown sugar, and simmer, stirring occasionally, until the sugar has been fully absorbed. **4.** Remove the syrup from the heat, pour into a sealable container, and let cool.

Assam Tea Syrup

Assam derives its name from the Assam region of India, the world's largest tea-growing region. A light and malty flavored black tea, it is the perfect blend to use to make our tea syrup. This syrup works particularly well when mixed with gin. Try adding the Assam syrup to a Tom Collins in place of the gomme to create an interesting twist on a classic.

YIELD
14 oz (410 ml)

INGREDIENTS
1 Assam tea bag

7 oz (210 ml) boiling water

7 oz (200 g) sugar

METHOD

1. Pour the boiling water over the tea bag and leave it to brew for 3 minutes, then discard the tea bag. 2. Add the brewed tea to a pan over medium heat, bring to a low simmer, and add the sugar. Continuously stir the mixture until the sugar has fully dissolved and the liquid has become transparent. 3. Remove the pan from the heat, let cool, then pour it into a bottle and store in the refrigerator.

GRENADINE

*T*his is a common syrup found in bars across the world and is an integral ingredient used in cocktail classics such as the Zombie, Singapore Sling, and Tequila Sunrise. Grenadine is a pomegranate syrup, which balances tart and sweet flavors.

— YIELD —

25 oz (740 ml)

INGREDIENTS

10.75 oz (322 ml) water

18 oz (510 g) pomegranate seeds

(scoop out from roughly 2 pomegranates)

1 lemon

12.5 oz (355 g) sugar

METHOD

1. Create a bain-marie by bringing a pan of water to a boil over high heat, then reduce to a simmer; rest a bowl or small pan on top with the base just touching the surface of the water. Add the water and pomegranate seeds to the empty pan, then cut the lemon, squeeze the juice into the same pan, and add the rind. 2. Lightly mash

the contents of the pan, ensuring the juice is released. Allow the mixture to simmer for an hour, then remove from the heat and strain through a muslin cloth. 3. Add the strained liquid to a clean pan over medium heat, add the sugar, and simmer, stirring occasionally, until all the sugar has been fully absorbed. 4. Remove the syrup from the heat, pour into a sealable container, and let cool.

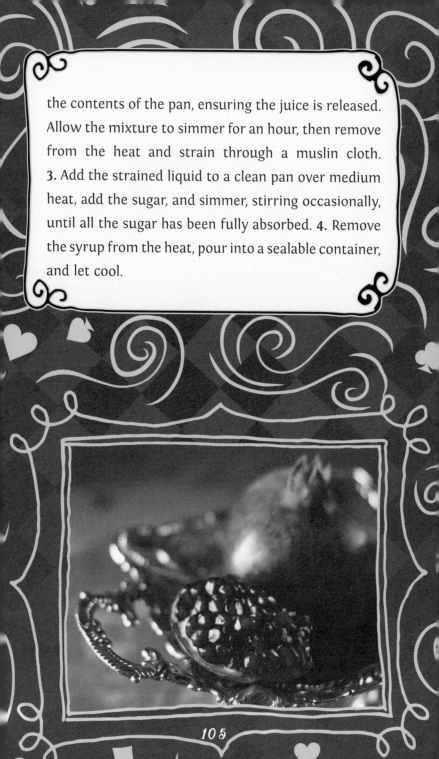

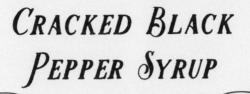

CRACKED BLACK PEPPER SYRUP

*T*his simple sugar syrup couples sweetness with the spice of cracked black pepper. We use this syrup to add the required spice and pepper flavors to our Duchess's Soup (page 60). It is a perfect syrup to partner with light fruits such as strawberry or watermelon. You can use this syrup to make a great watermelon and gin martini by muddling fresh watermelon and basil, then shaking with gin, citrus, and the syrup.

─ YIELD ─

14 oz (410 ml)

INGREDIENTS

7 oz (200 g) sugar

7 oz (210 ml) water

1 oz (28 g) cracked black pepper

METHOD

1. Bring the sugar, water, and cracked black pepper to a boil in a saucepan, simmer until all of the sugar

has dissolved into the water (2 to 3 minutes), stirring constantly. 2. Remove from heat, leave to cool, and retain in a clean, sealable bottle.

LIQUEURS

A wide range of liqueurs are readily available at most liquor stores and come in a large range of flavors. They are an easy way to add interesting flavor profiles to cocktails. If you have the time, though, there is nothing better than making your own homemade liqueurs. It's a great way to learn about the processes that go into making some of the most-loved cocktail ingredients, while also supplying yourself with a cost-effective alternative to buying a full range of liqueurs. Due to the alcohol content, these can be stored in a cool, dry pantry.

Orange Curaçao

A popular liqueur made with bitter orange peel, curaçao is a sweet digestive that was first made by the Dutch after discovering bitter oranges native to Curaçao, a Dutch West Indian island. Curaçao can be used in classic cocktails such as a Cosmopolitan, Mai Tai, and Sidecar.

YIELD

22.5 oz (665 ml)

INGREDIENTS

Peel from 2 oranges

Peel from 1 lemon

1 oz (28 g) Curaçao bitter orange peel

1 cinnamon stick

4 cardamom pods, cracked

2 whole cloves

9 oz (270 ml) vodka

13.5 oz (405 ml) simple sugar syrup (page 90)

METHOD

1. Add all the ingredients except the simple syrup to a mason jar, seal, and let steep for 2 weeks. **2.** Strain the mixture through a muslin cloth into a clean bowl, ensuring all peels and spices are removed. **3.** Add the simple syrup to the strained liquid, stir well, then pour into a bottle and seal.

Sweet Vermouth

Sweet vermouth is an essential ingredient in so many cocktails and should be a staple in every aspiring bartender's larder. Many quality brands are readily available, but this homemade recipe tastes delicious, and taking the time to make your own can elevate your cocktails to a whole new level, bringing an extra sense of accomplishment as another achievement is unlocked.

YIELD

25 oz (750 ml)

INGREDIENTS

1.75 oz (50 g) sugar

1 bottle (750 ml) pinot grigio

Peel from 1 orange

6 cardamom pods

2 star anise

1 teaspoon dried culinary lavender

1 teaspoon angelica root

½ teaspoon wormwood

½ teaspoon Curaçao bitter orange peel

1 teaspoon cinchona bark

1 teaspoon dried chamomile

1 cinnamon stick

2 oz (60 ml) boiling water

7 oz (210 ml) brandy

METHOD

1. Add the sugar to a large pan and melt over medium heat, stirring, until it turns a golden caramelized color. Remove from the heat and let cool. **2.** In a separate pan, combine 1 cup (240 ml) of the pinot grigio with the orange peel, spices, and herbs. Bring to the boil, reduce the heat, and simmer for 5 minutes with the lid on, then remove from the heat and strain through a muslin cloth into a clean pan. **3.** Carefully add the boiling water to the caramelized sugar, pouring it in slowly, stirring as you go. Be very careful because the caramelized sugar will be extremely hot and any splashes could scald your skin. **4.** Add the remaining pinot grigio to the herb-infused wine in the pan; stir and bring to a boil, then slowly pour this mixture into the caramelized sugar, still pouring slowly and cautiously. **5.** Finish the vermouth by adding the brandy to fortify it, let cool, then pour it into a bottle, seal, and store in the refrigerator.

DRY VERMOUTH

A simple adjustment to the previous recipe can allow you to make a very versatile dry vermouth; simply leave out the sugar and water. Mix together the herbal ingredients and wine in a pan, bring to a boil, then simmer with the lid on for 5 to 10 minutes. Allow the mixture to cool, then stir in the brandy and pour into a bottle.

INFUSED SPIRITS

*I*nfusing spirits at home is a great way to imbue your drink with unusual and exciting flavors. The readily available selection of flavored spirits is usually quite limited in range, so the advantage of infusing at home is that you can create a base spirit with any flavor you want. Therefore, get creative and start experimenting with a wide range of different combinations. Due to the alcohol content, these infused spirits can be stored in a cool, dry pantry.

Cucumber Vodka

Cucumber is a great flavor to pair with a grainy vodka, as it adds a fresh and subtle taste. Simply top this with tonic water and a slice of cucumber for a refreshing summer drink.

— YIELD —

12 oz (360 ml) vodka

INGREDIENTS

½ cucumber

2 sprigs cilantro

12 oz (360 ml) vodka

METHOD

1. Roughly chop the cucumber into small chunks, place in a 1-quart (1-L) mason jar, top with the vodka, and seal.
2. Leave the vodka to steep for a minimum of 3 days, before filtering out the cucumber and then carefully pouring the vodka infusion back into the bottle.

Vanilla Vodka

A great component for a range of dessert cocktails, add vanilla vodka to an espresso martini to create an extra layer of complexity.

YIELD

25 oz (750 ml)

INGREDIENTS

1 bottle (750 ml) vodka

2 vanilla pods

METHOD

1. Slice the vanilla pods lengthwise, scrape out the seeds, then place both the pods and the seeds into the bottle of vodka. Leave the mixture to steep for 3 days, then use a coffee filter to strain out the vanilla seeds. 2. Pour the vodka back into the bottle. If desired, add the seedless pod to the bottle and it will continue to infuse the liquid and create a stronger, more distinct vanilla flavor.

DARJEELING GIN

Darjeeling is floral tea that originates from the Darjeeling district of West Bengal, India. Mix with lemon juice and soda water for a sparkling, alcoholic iced tea.

— YIELD —

25 oz (750 ml)

INGREDIENTS

1 bottle (750 ml) gin

2 Darjeeling tea bags

METHOD

1. Pour the gin into a mason jar, add the tea bags, and seal. **2.** Leave the mixture to steep for 3 days, then fine strain the liquid into a bottle and store.

PUREE AND JUICES

P uree and juices add a wide range of flavors and textures to cocktails. Taking the time to prepare your own from fresh ingredients, rather than buying premade ingredients, will help to elevate the overall quality and flavor of your drinks. Once made, store these in a sealed container in a refrigerator for a maximum of three days.

BURNT PEACH PUREE

A thick, sweet puree, this is made by charring peach slices, which adds a depth of flavor that permeates through in our Curiouser and Curaçao cocktail (page 46). Simply scale up this recipe if you need to make larger quantities.

— YIELD —

About 3 oz (90 ml) peach puree

INGREDIENTS

1 ripe peach

Scant 1 oz (28 g) Demerara sugar

METHOD

1. Peel the peach and slice into 8 segments, discarding the pit. Toss the peach slices in the sugar, ensuring that each segment is well covered. 2. Lay the slices out on a griddle pan over medium heat and use tongs to regularly turn them. Cook for 5 minutes, or until the sugar has blackened and burned onto the peach segments. 3. Allow the caramel to cool, then reserve 2 slices for garnish before putting the remaining fruit into a food processor or blender and blitzing into a liquid. This will keep for up to 4 days in the refrigerator, or frozen for up to 30 days.

APPLE PUREE

A sweet puree used in our Digging for Apples (page 50), this works well with Calvados or whisky. You could stir it into an Old Fashioned to create a twist on this standard classic.

YIELD

About 14 oz (410 ml)

INGREDIENTS

2 large Gala apples

¾ oz (21 ml) sugar

1 cinnamon stick

7 oz (210 ml) boiling water

METHOD

1. Peel and core the apples, cut into small cubes, and add to a pan over medium heat. Add the sugar, cinnamon, and boiling water to the pan and simmer for 6 to 8 minutes, or until the apple is very soft. 2. Remove the mixture from the heat, remove the cinnamon stick, and blitz the mixture in a food processor until you have a smooth paste with no lumps.

BLOODY MARY MIX

*T*his classic Bloody Mary mix creates a trayful of our Pig and Pepper (page 58) shooters, or you can mix with vodka and a stick of fresh celery for the classic hangover cure.

— YIELD —

15 oz (440 ml)

INGREDIENTS

9 oz (270 ml) tomato juice

4.5 oz (135 ml) tomato puree

1.75 oz (52 ml) Worcestershire sauce

6 to 8 dashes Tabasco sauce

½ teaspoon celery salt

Cracked black pepper

1 tablespoon prepared horseradish

METHOD

1. Combine all the ingredients in a mason jar, cover, and store in the refrigerator; use within 3 days.

ICED TEA MIX

*T*his refreshing iced tea recipe can be stored in the fridge and enjoyed on a hot day, or alternatively used to mix our cocktail The Golden Afternoon (page 38).

YIELD
10 oz (300 ml)

INGREDIENTS
1 English breakfast tea bag

9 oz (270 ml) boiling water

0.5 oz (14 g) sugar

1 oz (30 ml) lemon juice

METHOD
1. Add the tea bag to the boiling water and let steep for 3 to 4 minutes, then discard the tea bag. **2.** Stir in the sugar and lemon juice and store in a mason jar in the refrigerator.

Fat-Washed Spirits

Fat-washing is a technique that is common in many bars around the world. Although it was first used by perfumers to extract aromas, it is now used in bars to infuse a spirit with complex, usual, and savory flavors. The process starts by first infusing a fat with a flavor. The fat then gets poured into a spirit to transfer the flavor to the spirit. The bottle of fatty spirit is then placed into a freezer to allow the fat to solidify. The solid layer of fat is removed and the alcohol is infused with the original ingredient flavor but without an overly fatty residue. Because a small amount of fat is left in the drink during the process, fat-washed alcohol is best stored in a sealed container in the fridge and should be consumed within a week.

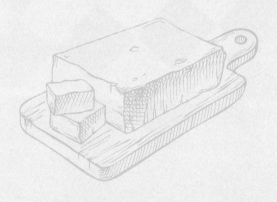

Buttered Toast— Infused Rum

T his is one of the many flavors Alice finds in the Drink Me potion and a firm favorite of ours (page 42); hot buttered toast.

YIELD
25 oz (750 ml)

INGREDIENTS
1 bottle (750 ml) rum

8 slices high-quality sourdough bread,
Cut ¼ inch (6 mm) thick

7 oz (200 g) high-quality unsalted butter

METHOD

1. Pour the contents of the rum bottle into a 1-quart (1-L) mason jar. This should fill up to around three-quarters of the jar, leaving plenty of space for the buttered toast!

2. Slowly toast your bread so that it is golden brown all over and brittle in texture. You may find that a low oven will achieve this better than a toaster can.

(continued on next page)

3. Make bread crumbs from the brittle toast in a food processor or by bashing with a rolling pin in a large bowl.

4. Melt the butter in a pan over low heat, taking care not to brown the butter. Add the bread crumbs to the pan and stir, allowing the bread to absorb the butter.

5. Once most of the butter has been absorbed by the crumbs, remove the pan from the heat and let the mixture cool slightly. You will not want to risk cracking the mason jar and letting your ingredients go to waste.

6. Once the buttered toast has cooled for a few minutes, use a spatula to add it to the mason jar with the rum, scraping every bit of butter and flavor from the pan. Seal the jar and shake hard for 30 to 60 seconds. Leave the flavors to infuse overnight.

7. Removing the toast at this stage will help with the later process of removing the butter. The toast flavor should be well and truly infused into the rum and butter. Remove the toast from the liquid by pouring through a fine strainer and pressing on the solids with a spatula or the back of a spoon. This will harden the butter while keeping the alcohol liquid.

8. The following day, line a funnel with a coffee filter or muslin cloth. Gradually pour the mixture through the filter and funnel into a second, clean container. Take your time with this part of the process, or you will risk losing valuable rum (and time!). Do not worry too much about removing every fragment of the butter from the rum, as the fat will be balanced by sharper flavors in the final cocktail and a smooth mouthfeel will be created.

9. Once you are happy with the resulting liquid, it can be rebottled for later use. Simply pour from the jar into the bottle, using the funnel (without the filter). Don't forget to label the bottle so that it is not mistaken for regular rum!

Note: You will notice that a portion of the rum has been lost to the ether; this loss is known in the distilling industry (here it is caused by evaporation) as The Angel's Share. This name is a rather cute one, and considering that it refers to loss of alcohol, some prefer the term The Devil's Cut.

VANILLA BEAN AND CAKE FROSTING—INFUSED VODKA

*T*his entry-level recipe is a simplified introduction to the technique of fat washing, and forms the spirit base for the Un-Birthday Cake Martini (page 84).

— YIELD —

25 oz (750 ml)

INGREDIENTS

1 bottle (750 ml) Cîroc vodka

1 vanilla bean

1 lemon (preferably unwaxed)

5.25 oz (150 g) vanilla buttercream cake frosting
(either homemade or store-bought will do the trick)

METHOD

1. Pour the entire contents of the vodka bottle into a mason jar. This should fill up to around three-quarters of the jar, leaving plenty of space for the remaining ingredients. 2. Score the vanilla bean lengthwise to allow the full flavor to be released into the vodka. Drop the vanilla bean into the vodka, along with any of the

spilled contents of the bean. **3.** Using a peeler, remove the zest from the lemon, taking care to avoid the bitter white pith. Drop this into the jar, too. Seal the jar and give it a good shake. Set aside for as long as you can, at least 24 hours. **4.** Dollop the buttercream frosting into a clean mason jar and pour the vanilla vodka over the top. Swirl the vodka around the frosting and leave to infuse overnight. **5.** At this stage, it's a great time to taste the final product—the sweetness of the buttercream should balance the sharpness of the lemon.

Note: Most buttercreams will dissolve into your vodka and the two will become one. Any solid pieces of frosting can be strained out with the lemon zest and vanilla pod, resulting in a sweet, smooth, creamy product, ready for drinking.

Pancetta and Pink Peppercorn Vodka

*A*dding meat flavors to drinks is one of the primary functions of fat-washing, and once you master the technique, it will open a whole new world of flavors for you to enjoy in your cocktails.

— YIELD —

10 oz (300 ml)

INGREDIENTS

9 oz (255 g) pancetta (or unsmoked bacon)

1 teaspoon pink peppercorns

10.75 oz (322 ml) vodka

METHOD

1. Add the pancetta to a dry pan over medium heat and cook for 5 minutes, or until it is crispy and all the fat has been released from the meat. **2.** Remove the pancetta from the pan with a slotted spoon, discard (or eat!) the pancetta, then add the peppercorns to the pan and toast them in the pancetta fat for 1 minute. Remove the pan from the heat, pour the remaining fat and peppercorns into a 1-quart (1-L) mason jar, top with the vodka, seal, and place in the freezer for 2 hours, or until the fat has fully separated and solidified at the top of the jar. 3. Remove the jar from the freezer and, using a spoon, scoop the layer of fat off the liquid. This process will remove the fat from the vodka but allow it to retain a smoky pancetta flavor. Ensure the peppercorns are still in the vodka and leave the sealed mason jar in a cool, dry place for 3 days to fully infuse the peppercorn flavor. 4. Use a sieve to filter out the peppercorns and any remaining pieces of fat and then pour the final vodka mixture back in its original bottle.

TURKEY RUM

Turkey, another meaty fat wash, has a relatively low fat content, so make sure to cook the meat thoroughly and that the butter soaks up the charred flavors. This flavor is a main ingredient in our Drink Me cocktail (page 42).

— YIELD —

25 oz (750 ml)

INGREDIENTS

10.75 oz (305 g) dark turkey meat (leg and thigh)

2.5 oz (70 g) salted butter

1 (750 ml) bottle golden rum

1. Cut the turkey meat into small chunks, then add the meat and the butter to a pan over medium heat. Cook the meat for 5 to 8 minutes, or until the meat is crispy and golden on the outside. Discard (eat!) the meat and allow the butter to cool. **2.** Pour the turkey butter into a 1-quart (1-L) mason jar and top with the golden rum. Place the mason jar in the freezer for 2 hours, or until the fat has fully separated and solidified at the top of the jar. **3.** Remove the jar from the freezer, then scoop the layer of fat off the liquid with a spoon. Finish by fine straining the rum into a bottle and storing in a cool, dark place.

DEHYDRATING FRUIT FOR GARNISH

Many ingredients can be dehydrated; soft and hard fruits work very well as cocktail garnishes and double as great snacks. Dehydrators can be purchased online reasonably cheaply, and the process with these machines is simple, mess free, and foolproof. If you plan on dehydrating large quantities of fruit, then invest in one; otherwise, use the following process and experiment with different fruits in various shapes and sizes.

You can dehydrate fruit by slicing into $\frac{1}{4}$-inch (6 mm) slices (or thinner) and baking for a few hours in a low oven. If you don't have access to a convection oven, you can use a conventional oven, but you may need to rotate the fruit for even dehydration. Apples, citrus fruit, and pineapple all work rather well, just be sure to wash your fruit thoroughly before dehydrating. Pat the fruit dry with a lint-free cloth, then lay out on baking sheets lined with parchment paper. Pop the sheets in your oven, on as low a temperature as it will go. The process may take a full day, but all the labor is over and done within a few minutes and the yield can be rather impressive. The following is an example of dehydrating fruit; smaller or larger pieces may need more or less time in your oven.

DEHYDRATED CITRUS WHEELS

The perfect garnish for a fresh, fruity cocktail, this garnish works particularly well in drinks made for highball, rocks, or coupe glasses.

INGREDIENTS

1 large pink grapefruit

METHOD

1. Slice a large pink grapefruit into wheels ½ inch (3 mm) thick. Lay the slices on a parchment paper–lined baking sheet. **2.** Put the sheet in the oven at the lowest temperature possible. Leave the fruit in the oven for 5 to 6 hours, turning each piece gently at the halfway point. **3.** Remove the fruit from the oven when it is completely dry and not tacky.

Note: Other fruits can be dehydrated using this method. Fruits such as apple and pear can discolor quickly, so combat this by rinsing and then dowsing with a splash of lemon juice.

ROASTED CITRUS ZEST

*T*his is a quick-and-easy garnish that is the perfect finish to many great cocktails. All citrus peels work equally well, and they can help elevate and complement the flavor of a drink while adding texture.

INGREDIENTS

1 citrus fruit

METHOD

1. Preheat the oven to 250°F (120°C). Finely grate the citrus peel onto a baking sheet. Place the sheet in the oven and bake for 8 to 10 minutes, or until the citrus is dry and crispy. **2.** Store in a mason jar in a cool, dry place.

CRISPY SAGE GARNISH

*L*ightly roasted herbs can add a lovely texture and scent to a drink, while being a beautiful final touch. We have used sage leaves for our Caterpillar's Hookah (page 54), but other roasted herbs such as rosemary or thyme can have a similar effect.

INGREDIENTS

1 sprig fresh sage

METHOD

1. Preheat the oven to 250°F (120°C). Pick the sage leaves from the stem, lay them on a baking sheet, and place the sheet in the oven for 8 to 10 minutes, or until the leaves are dry and crispy. **2.** The cripsy leaves will be very delicate, so store them carefully in a shallow container in a single layer to prevent crumbling.

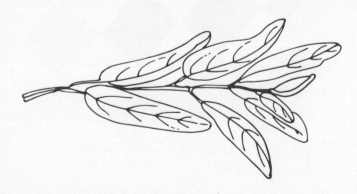

EPILOGUE

We hope that you have enjoyed your journey down the rabbit hole to discover our collection of Alice-based concoctions as much as we enjoyed creating the recipes themselves. We hope you feel confident enough to not only make the recipes as we have written them, but also to experiment with the drinks, manipulating them to suit your palate and home bar.

Until next time, stay curious.

Much love,
Nick and Paul

CONVERSION CHART

Fluid Ounces	Milliliters
0.25 (¼)	7
0.5 (½)	15
0.75 (¾)	22
1	30
1.5	45
2	60
3	90
4	120
5	150
6	180
7	210
8	240
9	270
10	300
11	330

1 teaspoon	5 ml

1 tablespoon	15 ml

RESOURCES

We recommend using search websites such as www.wine-searcher.com to find your closest supplier for cocktail ingredients. Listed below are the owners of all the brands we have used in our recipes, and their websites.

Edmond Briottet
www.briottet.fr

Quiquiriqui Mezcal
www.quiquiriquimezcal.com

Rémy Martin
www.remymartin.com

Paloma Drinks Company
www.palomadrinks.com

About the Authors

We are foremost good friends, brought together over a love of cocktails and a like-minded approach to flavor and taste. We both have spent many years in hospitality, managing some of London's best bars and restaurants before launching our own company, Paloma Drinks Company (www.palomadrinks.com). We organize pop-up events around the London while using our extensive knowledge to provide industry consultancy. With an appetite for unusual ingredients and unique flavor combinations, we wanted to get away from the cocktail fashions we came across in the 1990s: fluorescent, sickly sweet drinks served in giant receptacles, which invariably came partially frozen. Our reaction to this was to base many of our recipes on herbal flavors and unusual combinations of ingredients that would catch the eye on a menu, challenge the drinker's palate, and back it all up with a flavor to remember.